THE
TINY BOOK
of
TINY PLEASURES

Library of Congress Cataloging-in-Publication Data is available.
ISBN: 978-0-7611-9376-0

Design by Kat Millerick

Workman books are available at special discounts when purchased in bulk
for premiums and sales promotions as well as for fund-raising or educational
use. Special editions or book excerpts can also be created to specification.
For details, contact the Special Sales Director at the address below, or send
an email to specialmarkets@workman.com.

Workman Publishing Co., Inc.
225 Varick Street
New York, NY 10014-4381

workman.com
flowmagazine.com

FLOW® is a registered trademark of Sanoma Media Netherlands B.V.
WORKMAN is a registered trademark of Workman Publishing Co., Inc.

Printed in China
First printing March 2017

10 9 8 7 6 5 4 3 2 1

THE
TINY BOOK
of
TINY PLEASURES

Irene Smit and Astrid van der Hulst

Illustrated by
Deborah van der Schaaf

flow

WORKMAN PUBLISHING • NEW YORK

☐ HAVING A SIGNATURE STYLE

A TINY REMINDER

Always remember to look up once
in a while—a change in perspective,
no matter how small, can be magical.

☐ A RAINBOW

☐ A NEW ISSUE OF
YOUR FAVORITE MAGAZINE

☐ BUY ONE,
GET ONE FREE!

☐ BOOKING
A HOLIDAY

PACK YOUR BAGS

Most of the legends about the cheapest time to book a flight are not applicable to travel plans, or yield only small financial rewards. Instead, the most important factors are the days you plan on traveling. It's proven that Wednesday departures are often the cheapest, while Sunday departures can be the most expensive. On the way back from a domestic trip, Tuesday is usually cheapest, and a Wednesday return from an international trip will generally yield the best prices.

☐ GIVING AWAY SOMETHING
YOU DON'T USE ANYMORE

☐ THE BEST SEAT IN THE HOUSE

☐ FINDING MONEY
IN YOUR POCKET

☐ SHARING

Reading is the sole means by
which we slip, involuntarily,
often helplessly, into
another's skin, another's
voice, another's soul.

—Joyce Carol Oates

☐ A VERSE THAT TRANSPORTS

☐ A MANDARIN
WITH LEAVES

☐ UNEXPECTED LATTE ART

☐ TAKING YOUR BIKE,
INSTEAD OF A CAR

WHY RIDE A BIKE?

It's cheaper.
Maintaining a bike is about 30 times less
expensive per year than maintaining a car.

It's faster.
Bike trips of three to five miles can actually take
less or the same amount of time as traveling by
car because of the ability to avoid traffic jams.

It's healthy.
A year into biking to work, commuters on average
are 13 pounds lighter.

It's accessible.
Bike-sharing programs are popping up across
the country. Prices vary from city to city but
can be as low as $65 a year.

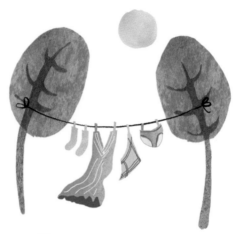

☐ HANGING THE LAUNDRY
OUTSIDE TO DRY

☐ A CHEERFUL UMBRELLA

☐ GREEN TRAFFIC LIGHTS
ALL THE WAY

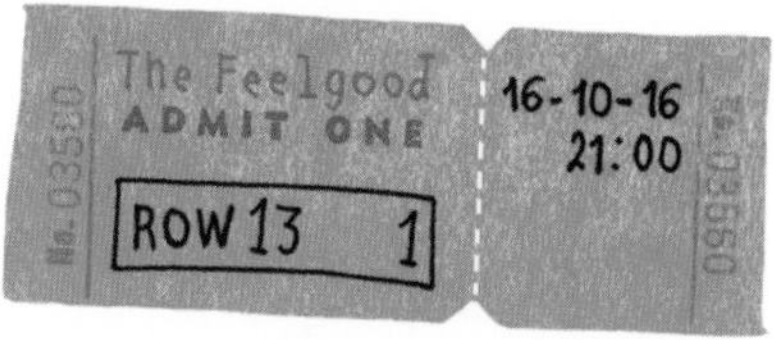

The Feelgood
ADMIT ONE
ROW 13   1

No. 03560

16-10-16
21:00

No. 03560

☐ GOING TO THE MOVIES

☐ PUTTING YOUR DREAMS TO PAPER

THINK BIG

A study shows that people who take the time to write down their goals or share status updates about those goals with a friend are much more likely to accomplish what they set out to achieve. Set aside some time each week to jot down your dreams and get ready to watch the magic happen.

☐ A PRIVATE JOKE

☐ A PLAYFUL SPIRIT

☐ A LONG, HOT BATH

INGREDIENTS FOR THE ULTIMATE BATH

Smell
Add bath salts for scented water.

Hear
Turn on a soothing playlist.

Touch
Pour a generous amount of bubble bath into
the running water for luxurious bubbles—
a classic for a reason.

Taste
Pour yourself a glass of your favorite beverage.

See
Grab a book or magazine that you've
been meaning to read but never seemed
to find the time.

☐ UNSCREWING A JAR
IN ONE GO

☐ ARMCHAIR TRAVEL

☐ AN UNEXPECTED DISCOUNT
AT THE CASH REGISTER

☐ HEARING THE WIND BLOWING
(WHILE YOU'RE <u>INSIDE</u>)

INSIDE THE CRYSTAL BALL

Some people believe that dreams hold the keys to our past, present, and future. Here are some other fields of fortune-telling that are believed to predict life events and personal characteristics.

Astrology
The study of the movements of the sun, moon, stars, and planets.

Numerology
The study of numbers attached to a person's name and date of birth.

Graphology
The study of handwriting.

Physiognomy
The study of facial features.

Phrenology
The study of the shape and size of the skull.

Palmistry
The study of lines on a person's palm.

☐ DREAMING A GOOD DREAM
AND WRITING IT DOWN

☐ HANGING GARLANDS UP
(JUST BECAUSE)

☐ FOREIGN CANDY WRAPPERS

☐ A DELICIOUS
  BREAKFAST

TOPPINGS FOR NEXT-LEVEL OATMEAL

Just Peachy
peaches + heavy cream

Out of the Gate
scrambled eggs + spinach + flax or hemp seeds

I Want S'mores
chocolate chips + graham cracker crumbs
+ mini marshmallows + brown sugar

Savory Sunrise
canned pumpkin + cottage cheese
+ toasted almonds

My Big Fat Greek Breakfast
Greek yogurt + berries + granola + maple syrup

Tropical Sunrise
unsweetened coconut + pineapple chunks
+ banana slices + chopped nuts

☐ A NOTE ON YOUR PILLOW

☐ BEING THE FIRST
TO DIP INTO THE JAR

☐ LEARNING A PHRASE IN
   ANOTHER LANGUAGE

HOW TO SAY "I LOVE YOU!" IN 10 DIFFERENT LANGUAGES

ALBANIAN: *Unë të dua!*

DUTCH: *Ik hou van je!*

FINNISH: *Minä rakastan sinua!*

FRENCH: *Je t'aime!*

GERMAN: *Ich liebe dich!*

INDONESIAN: *Aku cinta kamu!*

ITALIAN: *Ti amo!*

SPANISH: *Te amo!*

SWAHILI: *Nakupenda!*

VIETNAMESE: *Anh yêu em!*

☐

HELPING
SOMETHING
GROW

From the pit of
an avocado!

☐ LISTENING TO THE RADIO
OR YOUR FAVORITE PODCAST

☐ THINKING OF THE PRETTIEST
PLACE YOU KNOW

7 NATURAL WONDERS OF THE WORLD

Aurora Borealis
Most often found near the northern magnetic pole
(currently located near Canada's arctic islands)

Grand Canyon
United States

Great Barrier Reef
Australia

Harbor of Rio de Janeiro
Brazil

Mount Everest
In the Himalaya mountains between Nepal and Tibet

Parícutin
Mexico

Victoria Falls
The border between Zambia and Zimbabwe

☐ A NEW GO-TO RECIPE

☐ GETTING SOME FRESH AIR

☐ A TRAY FULL OF
HOMEMADE COOKIES

SIGNED, SEALED, AND DELIVERED

Homemade cookies are the perfect gift to make someone feel special. Go the extra mile with these creative packaging ideas:

* Line a patterned gift box with tissue paper and secure it with a rubber band—insert an ornament or embellishment underneath the band for an extra flourish.

* Fill a mason jar with cookies, alternating each with a square of festive baking paper for bursts of color.

* Decorate a tea tin with twine and a gift tag.

* Adorn a brown paper bag with washi tape, stickers, or stamps to dress up a classic.

☐ THE FINISHING TOUCH

☐ A DAY WITHOUT APPOINTMENTS

☐ A WORK OF ART

☐ OFFERING TO HELP

☐ RAINDROPS ON
THE WINDOWPANE

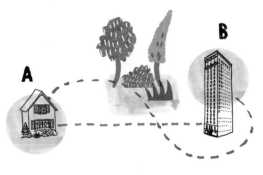

☐ TAKING AN UNEXPECTED ROUTE

☐ LOOKING UP AT THE SKY

THE SOUND OF SILENCE

Because there is no atmosphere in space, sound
waves don't have a medium to travel through,
making it completely silent out among the stars.

☐ A WILD WEEKEND!

☐ TOASTING GOOD NEWS
OR A GOOD PERSON

☐ A WELL-STOCKED
CUPBOARD

☐ DRESSING UP
  OR HAVING A
  COSTUME PARTY

FAMOUS ONSCREEN KISSES

Jack and Rose, *Titanic*

Noah and Allie, *The Notebook*

Kathryn and Cecile, *Cruel Intentions*

Rhett and Scarlett, *Gone With the Wind*

Jack and Ennis, *Brokeback Mountain*

Spider-Man and Mary Jane, *Spider-Man*

Paul and Holly, *Breakfast at Tiffany's*

Cecil and Gloria, *The Butler*

☐ A kiss

☐ DIVING INTO
A PHOTO BOOTH

☐ WARM BREAD

☐ CLICKING WITH SOMEONE

☐ DRIFTING OFF TO SLEEP

☐ A CHERISHED POSSESSION THAT REMINDS
YOU OF THE PERSON WHO GAVE IT TO YOU

☐ (SHAMELESS) SINGING
   IN THE SHOWER

CLEVER CONVERSATION STARTERS

* What's the best thing you've ever won?

* Describe the thing that always makes you laugh.

* What's the craziest thing you've ever done?

* If you could bring only three items to a deserted island, what would they be?

* What would you do if you won the lottery?

* If you could have dinner with a famous person, dead or alive, who would you choose (and what would you eat)?

☐ A FRIENDLY HELLO

☐ A LEISURELY BREAKFAST,
FIRST ON YOUR TO-DO LIST

☐ HANDS IN THE EARTH
(AND YOUR HEAD IN THE
CLOUDS)

BEAUTIFUL HELEN PEARS

Poires belle-Hélène is a French dish that consists of poached pears served with vanilla ice cream, chocolate sauce, and, in its fanciest iteration, crystallized violets. The beautiful dessert is said to be named after Jacques Offenbach's 1864 operetta *La belle Hélène*, a parody of events that led up to the Trojan War.

☐ POACHED PEARS
(AND THE SCENT OF CINNAMON)

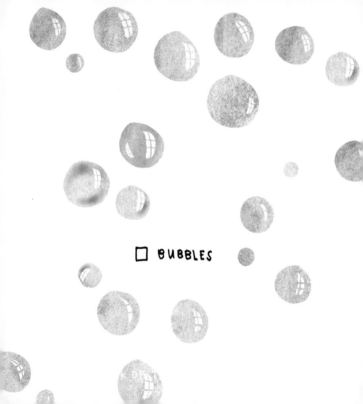

□ BUBBLES

□ CRAFTS YOU CAN EAT

☐ BIG THINGS WITH
   SMALL BEGINNINGS

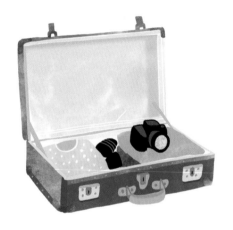

☐ ANTICIPATION

☐ A CHORUS AT DAWN

MUSIC TO OUR EARS

Gather some friends and warm up your vocal cords! Studies show that singing in groups has a warm, calming effect on those partaking in the activity. Singing requires slower breathing and results in a slower heart rate, which, coupled with the release of endorphins, produces an anxiety-reducing, pleasurable state. Not only that, group singing brings people together more efficiently than any other group activity, possibly due to its transcendence of language.

☐ BARE BRANCHES ETCHED
IN THE MOONLIGHT

☐ BEING THERE FOR SOMEONE
WHO NEEDS YOU

3 TRICKS FOR THE PERFECT FLIP

* Use a griddle or similar heavy-bottomed pan with the biggest width possible so there's enough room to flip without making a mess.

* Contrary to the mainstream belief that the mere appearance of bubbles means it's time to flip, the true indicator is actually when the bubbles start popping and forming craterlike holes on the top of the pancake.

* The final and most important step: Instead of using your whole arm to flip the pancake, slide a thin spatula underneath, lift it a few inches above the pan, and quickly turn your wrist. This technique cuts down on batter smears, but if you don't get it right the first time, not to worry—it still tastes the same, and practice makes perfect!

☐ A PERFECTLY
  FLIPPED PANCAKE

☐ BREAKFAST IN BED

☐ WARM BREATH
ON A CRISP DAY

☐ TAKING A SENTIMENTAL JOURNEY

☐ LOSING YOURSELF
IN A BOOKSHOP

☐ A SPA DAY

DIY HONEY CITRUS MASK

3 tablespoons orange juice

½ cup honey

1. In a small bowl, mix together
   the orange juice and honey.
2. Using your finger, apply the mixture
   to your face.
3. After 30 minutes, rinse your face with
   warm water followed by cool water.
4. Apply moisturizer to lock in your
   natural glow.

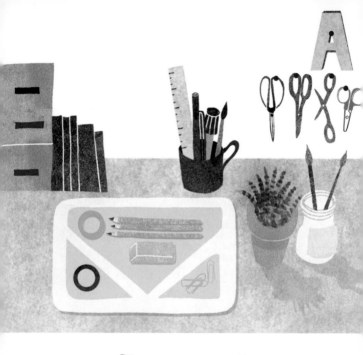

☐ A TIDY DESK

☐ THE ONLINE PURCHASE
ARRIVING AT YOUR DOOR

I have perceiv'd that to be with
those I like is enough.

—Walt Whitman

☐ FRIENDSHIP

☐ A SCARF TO
WRAP UP IN

☐ QUALITY CRAFTSMANSHIP

☐ UNPLUGGING FOR A WHILE

☐ SPLASHING IN PUDDLES

☐ A CHALK DRAWING ON THE SIDEWALK

FUN SIDEWALK GAMES

Hopscotch

Four square

Tic-tac-toe

Marbles

Scully

Jump rope

Jacks

Stoopball

☐ A CUP OF
COMFORT

☐ FEELING THE WIND IN YOUR HAIR

☐ A NEW FRIEND CRUSH

☐ A HOME AWAY FROM HOME

☐ AN EVENING OUT

☐ DRAWING ON A
FROSTY WINDOW

☐ FINDING FACES IN
EVERYDAY OBJECTS

☐ WARM HANDS

☐ A RESTFUL
NIGHT

☐ RAYS OF LIGHT SHINING ON THE WALL, JUST LIKE IN A HOPPER PAINTING

10 OF THE WORLD'S BEST ROAD TRIPS

The Garden Route, South Africa

South Island Circuit, New Zealand

Ring Road, Iceland

Tasmanian Peninsula, Australia

Highway 61, United States

The Atlantic Road, Norway

Basque Circuit, Spain

Ocean Drive, United States

Amalfi Coast, Italy

Karakoram Highway, Pakistan

☐ THE OPEN ROAD

☐ A QUIET SIDE STREET

☐ PEELING AN ORANGE
IN ONE GO

☐ APPRECIATING
WHAT YOU DO HAVE

IT'S A BEAUTIFUL LIFE

Studies show that expressing gratitude makes
you happy not only in the present but also in
the days, weeks, and months to come. Whether
you pen a sincere thank-you note or simply write
down moments of positivity, the results are the
same: Study participants experienced increased
happiness one month after their letter delivery,
and those who recorded positive life events for
a week felt the effects for six months.

☐ A BEAUTIFULLY LAID TABLE

□ SAYING NO FOR ONCE

☐ A MEAL THAT'S
EVEN BETTER
THE DAY AFTER

☐ AN EVENING OF CRAFTING

☐ WANDERING THROUGH A (NEW) CITY

THE WORLD'S MOST WALKABLE CITIES

Florence, Italy

Paris, France

Dubrovnik, Croatia

New York City, New York, United States

Vancouver, British Columbia, Canada

Edinburgh, Scotland

Boston, Massachusetts, United States

Melbourne, Australia

☐ GOING OUTSIDE
WITHOUT A COAT

☐ DARING TO DANCE

☐ GETTING A CALL FROM
SOMEONE YOU WERE
JUST THINKING ABOUT

☐ SHARING A COMFORTABLE SILENCE

☐ A SCENT FROM DAYS
GONE BY

TAKE A DEEP BREATH

Certain aromas can naturally influence your brain's chemistry as you carry out relaxing activities like reading, massage therapy, or meditation. Here are a few to try.

- Rosemary
- Peppermint
- Lemon
- Eucalyptus
- Thyme
- Jasmine
- Lavender

☐ AUTUMN LEAVES

☐ MAKING SOMETHING FROM SCRATCH

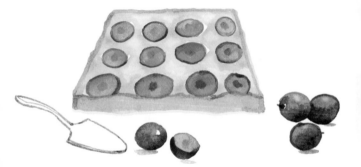

☐ SMALL AND
DELICIOUS BITES

☐ MAKING A WISH AND BLOWING ON A DANDELION PUFF

A CHANGE WILL DO YOU GOOD

☐ A MAKEOVER

HOME MAKEOVER TIPS THAT
DON'T COST ANYTHING

- Use old bracelets as napkin rings.

- Decorate drawer handles and knobs with ribbons.

- Create a headboard out of a quilt.

- Move furniture away from the wall to make a room seem larger.

- Use a scrap of fabric or large scarf to create a table runner.

- Turn a stack of books into a side table.

- Repurpose mismatched drinking glasses as vases.

☐ WOOLLY SOCKS

☐ SAVING OR FINDING SOMETHING
BETWEEN THE PAGES OF A BOOK

EASY MINDFULNESS EXERCISES

Watch your breath.
Breathe in through your nose and out through your mouth, following your breath as it travels. Let go of all stressful thoughts.

Observe your world.
Looking around you, find something that comes from nature, such as a plant, and focus on it. Notice every aspect of it and contemplate all that it does in connection to you and the outside world.

Cultivate awareness.
Every time you experience a negative thought, acknowledge that it is unproductive. Rather than letting it fester, dispel it from your mind.

☐ FINDING A MOMENT OF SERENITY

☐ FINDING SOMETHING
PRECIOUS IN YOUR BAG

☐ RELIABLE WINGMEN
(OR WOMEN)

☐ GETTING INSIDE JUST BEFORE THE RAIN STARTS

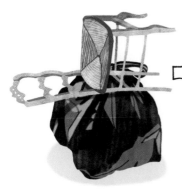

□ FINDING A TREASURE
ON THE STREET

☐ A TV SERIES OBSESSION

THE PROS OF BINGE-WATCHING

It feels good.
When you partake in fun activities—such as
binge-watching—the brain releases dopamine,
the neurotransmitter that produces pleasure.

It's smart.
You can easily keep track of plot intricacies,
and you'll be more likely to pick up on
Easter egg-nuances.

It's a way to connect.
When you watch a show with someone else,
it becomes a topic of conversation and
a way to spend time together.

□ TRYING A NEW INGREDIENT
AT YOUR LOCAL FARMERS' MARKET

☐ PUTTING AN END TO
A QUARREL

☐ A GREAT VIEW

WAYS TO GET A GREAT VIEW

- Climb a mountain (or take a chair lift or gondola).

- Take a hot-air balloon ride.

- Look out from a bridge.

- Climb the stairs (or take the elevator) to the top floor of a tall building.

- Hike around a national park.

- Relax on a beach and wait for the sunset.

- Go to the middle of nowhere and stargaze.

- Look at your loved ones.

☐ THE SHADE
OF A TREE

☐ A ROW OF DUCKLINGS

☐ LYING ON THE SOFA,
UNDER A BLANKET

YE AH

☐ AN ENTHUSIASTIC SUPPORT SYSTEM

Happiness can be found,

even in the darkest times, if one

only remembers to turn on the light.

—J. K. Rowling, *Harry Potter and the Prisoner of Azkaban*

☐ LIGHTING CANDLES

☐ CRISP,
CLEAN
BEDSHEETS

☐ FINDING SOMETHING FOR YOUR COLLECTION

☐ A TOADSTOOL

☐ AN EVENING STROLL

☐ AN EXTRA-LARGE
POPCORN

• A caller reported at 7:14 p.m. that someone was standing on the porch of a residence on Bank Street, yelling for help. Officers responded and learned that the person was, in fact, calling for their cat named "Help."

☐ FUNNY NEWS

☐ WARM FEET

☐ THE SOUND OF SILENCE

☐ AN INSPIRED
CREATION

UNLEASH YOUR IMAGINATION

Warren Buffett, one of the most successful
businessmen and inventors in the world, has
famously stated that he dedicates approximately
80 percent of each workday to
reading and thinking.

A HAND TO HOLD

Humans aren't the only ones who appreciate a familiar touch!

* Sea otters hold hands as they float so they aren't separated by the water's current.

* Elephants often wind their trunks together to show affection.

* Anteater babies get a piggyback ride on top of their mother for the first year of their life as a protective measure.

* During courtship, seahorses can be found linking tails and swimming with their snouts pressed together.

☐ A HUG

☐ SPRINKLES!

7 WAYS TO SAY "SPRINKLES"

What's in a name? That we call sprinkles by any other name would taste as sweet . . .

* Nonpareils

* Confetti

* Pearl dragées

* Sanding sugar

* Jimmies

* Hundreds-and-thousands

* *Muisjes* (Dutch: "little mice")

☐ A CHILD'S DRAWING

☐ A TREE IN
BLOOM

☐ FALLING DOWN A RABBIT HOLE
OF INSPIRATION

☐ STEPPING INTO A NICE WARM HOUSE WHEN IT'S COLD OUTSIDE

☐ EMBRACING WANDERLUST

KAUKOKAIPUU:

A Finnish word to describe the feeling of being homesick for a place you've never been

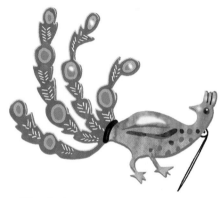

☐ FINDING SOMETHING YOU LOST

♡142 ⎘2

☐ FEELING THE LOVE

☐ THINKING ABOUT WHAT
   YOU'RE GOOD AT

RISK AND REWARD

If you want to get better at something, you have to step out of your comfort zone. Studies dating back to 1908 consistently support the idea that improvement requires some anxiety. The trick is to strike the right balance: Too much unease can make you feel stuck; too little, and you lose your motivation.

☐ BIRD FOOTPRINTS
   IN THE SNOW

☐ CATCHING UP ON
YOUR FAVORITE SHOW

☐ THE WEEKEND
PAPER

☐ THE SCENT OF
CLEAN LAUNDRY

☐ BEAUTIFULLY DRESSED
OLDER LADIES

Fashion you can buy, but style you possess. The key to style is learning who you are, which takes years. It's about self-expression and, above all, attitude.

—Iris Apfel

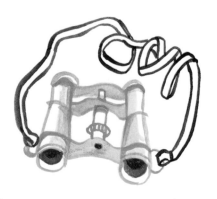

☐ LOOKING AT SOMETHING
THROUGH A NEW LENS

☐ GOING TO OR GIVING A CONCERT

☐ FLIRTING A BIT

☐ A CANDLE WHEN
THE POWER GOES OUT

☐ A CONTENTED GUEST

WELCOME, FRIENDS

If you're hosting visitors, here are a few tips to make them feel extra loved and comfortable.

- Fill a vase with fresh flowers and place it in their room or the kitchen.

- Set out a clean glass with a bottle or pitcher of water.

- Invest in a few mini toiletries and stash them in the bathroom.

- Stack a few current magazines or books on the shelf or bedside table.

- Place a chocolate on the pillow!

☐ WAKING UP TO FRESH SNOW

☐ EMBRACING YOUR
INNER CHILD

☐ ~~BAKING~~ EATING A CAKE

☐ REMEMBERING THOSE
VACATION VIBES

☐ ARRANGING YOUR PENCILS /
CLOSET / BOOKSHELF BY COLOR

☐ WEARING A HAT
WITH GRACE AND STYLE

☐ LOSING YOURSELF IN
SOMETHING

EMBRACE THE DAYDREAM

A study showed that engaging in mindless
or repetitive activities resulted in a surge in
inspiration and improved problem-solving
skills, so don't feel guilty about letting your
mind wander—it's probably taking
you somewhere interesting.

☐ MAKING A DAISY CHAIN

☐ DRIVING WITH MUSIC ON AND
WINDOWS OPEN

☐ A BUMBLEBEE DRINKING NECTAR
FROM A FLOWER IN THE GARDEN

SAVE THE BEES!

As pollinators, bees are vital to a beautiful garden. Here are some tips for attracting them:

* Plant a variety of native wildflowers that differ in size, shape, and seasonality.

* Choose flowers with purple, yellow, white, or blue petals.

* Leave about 3 to 4 feet between plants.

* Don't use pesticides.

* Create nesting spaces in the dirt.

* Cut back on the manicuring to allow flower growth.

☐ SOMETHING FRESH OUT OF
THE OVEN

☐ A FIT OF THE
GIGGLES

☐ THE SCENT OF FRESHLY MOWED GRASS

☐ EATING LOCAL OR
SEASONAL FARE

☐ A PURRING CAT

GOOD VIBRATIONS

There's good reason to love the deep, melodic rumbling sound of a cat purring. Studies have shown that, beyond the soothing qualities of the sound, purring has physical health benefits, too: The sound frequency at which cats purr (between 25 and 50 hertz) improves bone density and promotes healing in both cats and their humans. Scientists hypothesize that purring plays a key role in the relatively sedentary lifestyle of cats—felines spend so much time conserving energy (sleeping upward of 16 hours a day), that purring might also be a mechanism that stimulates muscles and bones without using much energy.

☐ LOOKING THROUGH
OLD FAMILY PHOTOS

☐ SHELLING YOUR
OWN PEAS

☐ BILLOWING SUMMER
DRESSES

☐ PICNIC TIME

PUT ON THE KETTLE!

Studies show that regularly enjoying a cup of tea leads to lower stress levels. Experts believe this relaxing effect is due to the amino acids found in green and black teas.

☐ DRINKING TEA OUT
   OF A BEAUTIFUL
   CHINA CUP

☐ CREATING SOMETHING

☐ DAYDREAMS

☐ SPOTTING A BIRD'S NEST

Have nothing in your houses that
you do not know to be useful, or
believe to be beautiful.

—William Morris

☐ AN AFTERNOON
SPENT LISTENING
TO OLDIES

☐ STAYING IN BED FOR AS
LONG AS YOU LIKE

☐ LICKING THE MIXING
BOWL CLEAN

☐ A POSTCARD THAT
CHEERS YOU UP, PINNED
ABOVE YOUR DESK

DIY SMILING POTS

To add some personality to your space, find a small terracotta pot and paint it white. Once it's dry, sketch out a facial expression in pen or pencil. When you're satisfied with the face, go over the sketch lines with permanent black marker or use a paintbrush and black paint. Add a plant and watch your happiness grow.

☐ GREENERY

☐ DECORATING
A SMALL CORNER
OF YOUR LIFE

☐ BREATHING IN NATURE

こんにちは

ko n ni chi wa

Hello

はじめまして

ha ji me ma shi te

Nice to meet you

☐ LEARNING SOMETHING NEW

BRAIN TRAINING

A study showed that the key to keeping your brain sharp and improving memory is to learn a new skill, whether it's quilting, photography, or playing an instrument. Engaging in a challenging activity strengthens the connections in the brain, which keeps you from aging mentally.

☐ SPOTTING SOMETHING
BEAUTIFUL

☐ FRESH-SQUEEZED LEMONADE

☐ A SHARP POINT ON
YOUR PENCIL

☐ A ROMANTIC GESTURE

OUTDOOR THERAPY

Absorbing the sights and sounds of nature
is more beneficial than you might think.
The Japanese practice of *shinrin-yoku*—
translated as "taking in the forest" or "forest
bathing"—is proven to reduce stress and
boost relaxation and overall vitality.

☐ TAKING A SHORT WALK
IN THE WOODS

□ A DAY IN THE PARK

☐ JUST CATCHING THE BUS
(OR TRAIN/METRO/TRAM)

☐ A FRESH START

☐ A SUCCULENT WATERMELON

☐ A WHISTLING KETTLE

HOW TO CURE STRESS WITH SOUND

A survey that polled adults on what sounds they found most relaxing showed that noises associated with food are among those that are most comforting, helping to lower stress and maximize relaxation. So the next time you need to decompress, trade in the ocean waves for one of these sounds:

* Sizzle of bacon

* Glug of wine pouring from a bottle

* Beer or soda can opening

* Barbecue crackling on a grill

* Toaster popping

* Teakettle whistling

* Champagne cork releasing

☐ CATCHING A SNOWFLAKE
ON YOUR TONGUE

 □ READING IN BED

☐ FRIENDS WHO APPRECIATE
YOUR QUIRKS

STRENGTH IN NUMBERS

You are 50 percent more likely to live longer if
you have a wide network of strong friendships.

☐ FINISHING A TASK

EXQUISITE

☐ A BEAUTIFUL WORD

☐ THE LAST GOOEY SIP
OF HOT CHOCOLATE

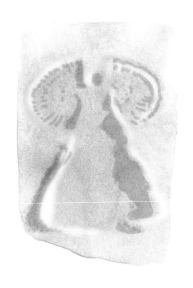

☐ A SNOW ANGEL

□ A LOCAL FAIR

CANDIED CINNAMON NUTS

Makes about 2 cups

Butter, for greasing the baking sheet
1 large egg white
1/2 cup granulated sugar
1 teaspoon freshly ground nutmeg
1 teaspoon freshly ground cinnamon
1/2 teaspoon salt
2 cups nut halves (try pecans, walnuts, or peanuts)

1. Preheat the oven to 300°F. Lightly coat a large baking sheet with butter.
2. In a small bowl, whisk the egg white until it becomes foamy. Add the sugar, spices, and salt and continue whisking until the mixture turns thick. Add the nuts and stir until they're completely coated in the mixture.
3. Transfer the nuts to the prepared baking sheet, allowing any excess mixture to drip off into the bowl before placing them on the baking sheet. Use a fork to space them out on the baking sheet.
4. Bake until the nuts turn golden brown, about 35 minutes. Cool completely before serving.

☐ A WALK WITH A
(FURRY) FRIEND

☐ WEARING SOMETHING BRIGHT
ON A GRAY DAY

☐ FERN FROST ON
A WINDOW

☐ A MEAL THAT HAS BEEN
COOKED FOR YOU

☐ AN INDIAN SUMMER

A BLACKBERRY WINTER

The seasonal opposite of an Indian summer is
a cold snap that happens in late spring,
commonly referred to as a "blackberry winter,"
because this weather was believed to help
blackberries start growing in the North American
South and Midwest. It is often referred to by
other colloquial names derived from regional
blooms, such as dogwood winter, locust winter,
and whippoorwill winter.

☐ A SUNNY DAY
TO YOURSELF

☐ WONDERFULLY
   KITSCHY SOUVENIRS

☐ CLIMBING A MOUNTAIN
(LITERALLY OR
FIGURATIVELY)

A PICTURESQUE PANORAMA

Volcán Barú, the highest peak in Panama measuring 11,398 feet (3,474 meters), offers more than just an adventurous hike and spectacular view. If you make it to the top on a clear day, you'll see the Atlantic Ocean to the east and the Pacific Ocean to the west—the very definition of a picture worth a thousand words.

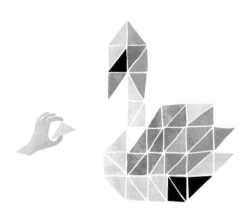

☐ SOLVING A PROBLEM OR
TALKING IT THROUGH

☐ A PRE-WARMED BED

☐ FLIP-FLOP WEATHER

☐ FINDING
THE WORDS YOU
WERE LOOKING FOR

☐ A SMALL BIT OF PRAISE

HOW TO SAY "GOOD JOB!"
IN 10 DIFFERENT LANGUAGES

ALBANIAN: *Punë e mirë!*

DUTCH: *Goed gedaan!*

FINNISH: *Hyvää työtä!*

FRENCH: *Bon travail!*

GERMAN: *Gut gemacht!*

INDONESIAN: *Kerja bagus!*

ITALIAN: *Buon lavoro!*

SPANISH: *Buen trabajo!*

SWAHILI: *Kazi nzuri!*

VIETNAMESE: *Làm tot lam!*

☐ A BUTTERFLY FLITTING
IN THE SUN

□ A FLEA MARKET SCORE!

☐ WATCHING A CLASSIC FILM
AGAIN (AND AGAIN AND
AGAIN AND AGAIN ...)

☐ PRINTING YOUR PHOTOS

THE WORLD'S TALLEST SANDCASTLE

In 2015, Ted Siebert, along with a crew of expert sand sculptors commissioned by Turkish Airlines, constructed the tallest sandcastle ever built at 45 feet and 10.25 inches (14 meters). The feat took place over a period of two weeks in Miami, Florida, using 1,800 tons (1,633 metric tons) of sand.

☐ BUILDING A
SANDCASTLE

☐ THE SCENT OF CITRUS

□ A PAGE TO COLOR

☐ A GOOD-LOOKING
   PASSPORT PHOTO!

☐ WARM TEA

SWEET DREAMS

The old-fashioned adage of counting sheep has been around forever—but does it really work? Researchers at Oxford University tested it out, only to discover that subjects who imagined peaceful imagery were able to fall asleep 20 minutes sooner than those who were instructed to use a distraction technique, such as counting sheep.

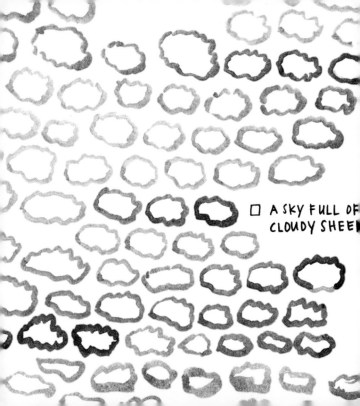

☐ A SKY FULL OF CLOUDY SHEEP

☐ A SMALL GESTURE

☐ THE MUSIC OF GRASSHOPPERS

☐ A WELL-DOCUMENTED
ADVENTURE

SUMMER BUCKET LIST

* Take a hike

* Go on a road trip

* Run through the sprinklers

* Make s'mores

* Go strawberry picking

* Try out a new beach

* Watch a movie at the drive-in

* Have a water-balloon fight

□ AN EPIPHANY

☐ TIDYING UP YOUR
MIND OR HOME

☐ MARSHMALLOWS MELTING
IN YOUR HOT CHOCOLATE

☐ PUTTING THE TENT UP IN ONE GO

WHEN YOU PUT UP A TENT...

. . . you eventually have to take it down. Similar to folding a fitted sheet, getting a tent back into its bag is often a perplexing endeavor. What most people don't realize is that tent bags are made to fit the tent poles. The simple trick: Fold your tent to match the length of your tent poles. Then simply place the poles at one end of the tent, roll them up, and slide the tent into the bag.

☐ A COMPLIMENT

☐ A BLANK DIARY

☐ QUALITY TIME

HOW TO SHARE A HOME WITH PETS

To make the most of a snuggle session with a furry friend, keep these tips in mind when choosing furniture and home accessories.

* If you want to hide pet hair, look for fabrics with patterns—hair tends to be less noticeable against busier prints, especially if they are the same color as the hair.

* For furniture that's easy to clean, your best bet is synthetic fiber. Scratches and marks can simply be brushed away, and if the upholstery is coded "W," all that's needed for a good wipe-down is soap and water.

* Don't forget to treat any new furniture with a fabric and upholstery protective spray, which helps battle liquids and stains and can be used on most materials.

☐ SOMETHING THAT
FALLS YET DOESN'T
BREAK

☐ THE FIRST BLOOMS
OF SPRING

☐ POPPIES

☐ GOING TO
THE BEACH

☐ SPOONING

HUG IT OUT

Research shows that the mere act of embracing—whether it's a partner, a friend, or a pet—releases oxytocin in our brains, making us happier and less stressed.

Without you the universe is not beautiful.

☐ TEA BAG WISDOM

☐ GREETINGS FROM
A FARAWAY FRIEND

☐ READING A BOOK

☐ READING ANOTHER BOOK

☐ HUNTING FOR SEASHELLS

A BEACHY TREASURE HUNT

Keep an eye out for these rare finds when combing the beach for beautiful shells.

* Shark teeth
* Pearls
* Whole sand dollars
* Red or blue sea glass
* Sea beans
* Arrowheads

☐ PRETTY PACKAGING

☐ OLD LOVE

☐ WILD
STRAWBERRIES

CHOCOLATE-COVERED STRAWBERRIES

Makes about 20 strawberries

1 pound (about 20) strawberries
4 ounces semisweet chocolate

1. Line a baking sheet with wax paper and set
   aside, then wash and dry the strawberries.

2. Chop the chocolate into coarse chunks and
   place them in a small heatproof bowl. Melt
   the chocolate in the microwave for 30-second
   intervals, stirring in between each, until it
   reaches a smooth consistency.

3. Dip each strawberry into the melted chocolate
   and place them on the baking sheet. Put
   the strawberries in the refrigerator until the
   chocolate hardens, about 30 minutes.

☐ RELAXING AFTER
A LONG DAY

□ HEADING FOR THE SEA

☐ MORNING DEW

☐ COLLECTING TICKETS, FLOWERS,
AND OTHER THINGS FOR YOUR
VACATION SCRAPBOOK

☐ BUYING AN ICE CREAM CONE WITH
ONE MORE SCOOP THAN YOU INTENDED

STRANGEST ICE CREAM FLAVORS
EVER CREATED

Lobster
Ben & Bill's Chocolate Emporium, Bar Harbor, Maine

Spaghetti and cheese
Heladeria Coromoto, Venezuela

Merlot
Max and Mina's, Queens, New York

Bacon
The Ice Cream Store, Rehoboth Beach, Delaware

Foie gras
Philippe Faur, France

Sweet corn and blue cheese
Sweet Republic, Scottsdale, Arizona

☐ WRITING WITH YOUR FAVORITE PEN

□ A GOOD
HAIR DAY

☐ MIGRATING GEESE IN
V FORMATION

ANIMALS THAT SHARE
STRONG FAMILY BONDS

Rattlesnakes

Prairie dogs

Elephants

Orca whales

Chimpanzees

Otters

☐ COOKING AND EATING OUTSIDE

Echinacea purpurea

☐ SEEING A FLOWER AND KNOWING ITS NAME

□ SIESTA

THE ART OF NAPPING

Sleep researchers have found that, due to the nature of sleep cycles, certain time increments are better than others when taking a nap.

To refresh and reboot
10 to 20 minutes

To improve memory processing
60 minutes

To increase emotional and procedural memory and creativity
90 minutes

☐ A NIGHTTIME DIP

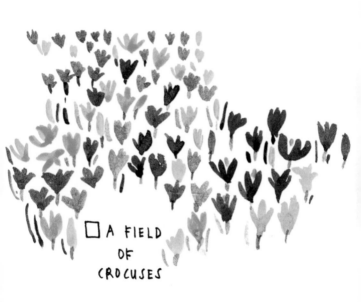

☐ A FIELD
OF
CROCUSES

☐ SENDING OR GETTING
SNAIL MAIL

☐ PARKING THE CAR IN ONE GO

☐ GLIMPSES OF NATURE
IN THE CITY

BEST US CITIES FOR NATURE LOVERS

San Francisco, California

Boston, Massachusetts

New York, New York

Washington, D.C.

Minneapolis, Minnesota

Philadelphia, Pennsylvania

Seattle, Washington

Chicago, Illinois

Milwaukee, Wisconsin

Oakland, California

☐ DOING SOMETHING YOU
NEVER DARED TO DO
BEFORE

(yes you can!)

☐ COMING HOME

☐ THE SMELL OF RAIN

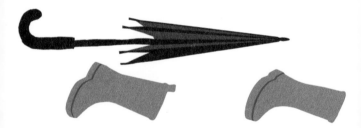

THE SILVER LINING

The smell of rain is just one of life's intangible, inexplicable pleasures—but there's actually a scientific explanation behind why people appreciate the scent. Chemical reactions occur when rain hits the ground that cause aromatic compounds—called petrichor—to release, which fill the air and make a rainy day more pleasant.

☐ HOMEMADE JAM

☐ READING (OR LEAFING THROUGH)
A FOREIGN NEWSPAPER

☐ SIPPING FROM YOUR
FAVORITE MUG

SPICE UP YOUR HOT CHOCOLATE

Add a fun twist to the chocolate-y classic
with these toppings.

Winter Mint
crushed candy canes + marshmallow fluff
+ peppermint extract

On Fire
cinnamon + cayenne pepper

Sweet and Salty
caramel sauce + salt

Chai Delight
ginger + cinnamon + cardamom

☐ YOUR FAVORITE
TRACK ON REPEAT

☐ EXPLORING YOUR OWN NEIGHBORHOOD

☐ READING TO SOMEONE

☐ A SUMMERTIME FIRE

☐ COLORS THAT
BRIGHTEN UP
A GRAY DAY

DIFFERENT HUES FOR
DIFFERENT HUMORS

It's commonly known that people
associate colors with emotions (yellow is happy),
symbols (green means rebirth), and judgments
(purple is regal). In an extension of this, different
parts of the brain fire up in the presence
of various colors, which, in turn, influence
how we perform. If you're feeling creatively
stifled, for example, consider spending some
time around the color blue.

☐ A LITTLE SOMETHING,
BEAUTIFULLY WRAPPED

☐ A SOLO
DANCE PARTY

☐ PLUCKING AN APPLE
FROM THE TREE

AN APPLE A DAY

All apples are good for you, but certain types
are best suited for cooking, baking, and eating.
Whether you're making a pie or just looking for
a snack, be sure to look for these types in the
field or at the store.

Best for baking
Braeburn, Jonagold, Cortland

Best for cooking
Granny Smith, Empire, Cameo

Best for eating
Honeycrisp, Gala, Red Delicious

☐ A BOWL OF
FRESH BERRIES

☐ A DAY IN THE GARDEN

☐ A ROAD TRIP

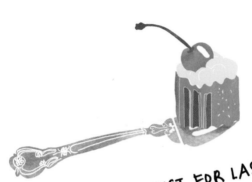

☐ SAVING THE BEST FOR LAST

☐ AN UNEXPECTED
LOVE NOTE

STRENGTH IN A STRANGER'S WORDS

In 2011, Hannah Brencher started The World Needs More Love Letters, an online organization that allows people to nominate loved ones in need of extra strength, courage, or affection. Strangers can sign up to receive these requests and handwrite their own letters, which are then delivered via snail mail to the person in need. Since its inception, letters have been mailed to all 50 states and across 6 continents. To nominate someone or write a love letter, visit moreloveletters.com.

□ CATCHING UP WITH A FRIEND

☐ REDISCOVERING A FORGOTTEN
   ITEM OF CLOTHING IN YOUR CLOSET

A LUCKY BREAK

If you've ever crossed your fingers or knocked on wood, consider yourself lucky! A study conducted by the University of Cologne in Germany discovered that those who believed in superstitions or good-luck charms had increased self-confidence and, consequently, performed better in a variety of situations.

☐ A LADYBUG ON YOUR HAND

☐ CHERRY BLOSSOMS

☐ SPONTANEOUS CHATS
WITH STRANGERS

☐ SITTING ON
A TERRACE

☐ A BOUQUET OF
WILDFLOWERS

☐ A COCKTAIL UMBRELLA
  IN YOUR DRINK

EASY HOMEMADE DAIQUIRI

Makes 1 drink

½ ounce strained, freshly squeezed lime juice

1 teaspoon granulated sugar

2 ounces white rum

1. Combine the lime juice and sugar in a mixing glass and stir to dissolve the sugar.
2. Add the rum, fill the glass three-quarters full with ice cubes, and shake vigorously until thoroughly chilled, 15 seconds.
3. Strain into a martini glass.

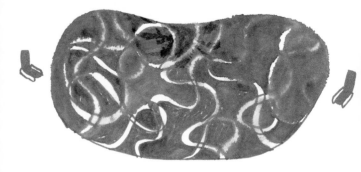

☐ SUNLIGHT REFLECTING OFF WATER

☐ A PEONY

A QUICK DIP

There are many factors that make up the perfect beach—white sand, warm waves, pristine views, and clear water, to name a few. The Persian Gulf checks all of those boxes, and with water temperatures climbing higher than 90°F in the summer, it is known as the warmest body of water on Earth.

☐ STANDING BAREFOOT
ON WARM SAND

☐ THE WAXING MOON

Supermarket Souvenir

PASTA DENTIFRIGA
Couto

☐ VISITING AN EXOTIC SHOP IN
YOUR NEIGHBORHOOD (AND
BRINGING BACK A SOUVENIR!)

☐ FINDING AND PLANTING SOME SEEDS

10 EASY PLANTS TO GROW

Lettuce

Cucumbers

Radishes

Snap peas

Basil

Green beans

Carrots

Beets

Thyme

Cilantro

☐ BRIGHTENING
SOMEONE'S DAY

☐ A SHARED MEAL

☐ FINDING YOUR CENTER

HANG (OUT) IN THE BALANCE

Deep breathing is scientifically proven to lower anxiety and has numerous other health benefits. But odds are that right now, you're breathing shallowly, or with your chest. When our bodies think we are short of breath, they trigger our sympathetic nervous system (which controls our "fight or flight" response), making us tense.

Take a moment to break the cycle and practice deep breathing. When you're in a calm place, try breathing in through your nose for four seconds, then breathe out through your nose or mouth—whichever feels more comfortable—for four seconds. Notice your heartbeat slow and your muscles relax. Repeat.

☐ CUTTING OUT
(AND PASTING UP)
A PRETTY PICTURE

☐ FINDING SOMETHING
TO CELEBRATE!

☐ STROLLING THROUGH A
STREET FESTIVAL

☐ A SILENT PHONE

bibimbap

☐ TASTING SOMETHING NEW

SUPERTASTERS

The average person has somewhere
between 2,000 and 8,000 taste buds. But
some people, known as supertasters, can
have up to twice as many. This means
that they taste all flavors—sweet, salty,
bitter, sour, or umami—more intensely, but
particularly bitter flavors. Supertasters
comprise about a quarter of the population
and are more likely to be women.

☐ A WISH

☐ A QUIET MORNING

☐ DRAWING OR PAINTING

EVERYDAY MASTERPIECES

The act of doodling is proven to sharpen focus, improve memory, and increase creative improvisation. Put your pencil to paper and let the ideas flow.

☐ A CAT NAP

☐ A GUILTY PLEASURE

☐ A FINISHED TO-DO LIST

HOW TO MAKE A BETTER TO-DO LIST

Anyone with a to-do list knows how satisfying it is to cross something off of it. Increase your productivity (and your feeling of accomplishment) by making the most of your list. Here are some tips to try.

* Your list should have no more than 10 tasks on it for a single day.

* Carve out some time every night to write your to-do list for the next day.

* Add "if then" action points to your list—if it's Friday morning, then I will complete task A.

* Start the list with the two most important tasks that absolutely need to get done that day.

* Make each task as specific as possible.

☐ A NEW PERSPECTIVE

☐ MAKING MISCHIEF

☐ FIREFLIES

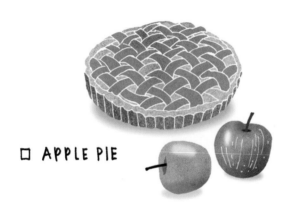

□ APPLE PIE

SOURCE LIST

p. 49: realsimple.com; brit.co; p. 84: bonappetit.com;
p. 91: marieclaire.com; p. 135: styleathome.com; bhg.com;
p. 224: delightfully-tacky.com; p. 251: bonappetit.com;
p. 309: realsimple.com; p. 363: *The 12 Bottle Bar* by David
Solmonson and Lesley Jacobs Solmonson

ABOUT THE AUTHORS

Irene Smit and Astrid van der Hulst are the cofounders and creative directors of *Flow* magazine, a popular international publication packed with paper goodies and beautiful illustrations that celebrate creativity, imperfection, and life's little pleasures. Astrid and Irene began their magazine careers as editors at *Cosmopolitan* and *Marie Claire*. In 2008, inspired by their passion for paper and quest for mindfulness, Irene and Astrid dreamed up the idea for their own magazine in a small attic and haven't looked back since. They live with their families in Haarlem, Netherlands.

ABOUT THE ILLUSTRATOR

Deborah van der Schaaf is a Dutch illustrator who graduated from the Willem de Kooning Academy in 2002. Since then, she has created art for various newspapers, magazines, and publishing houses, including *Flow* magazine, *Elle*, and *The Volkskrant*. Whether she's crafting, collaging, or painting with watercolors, Deborah is inspired by finding joy in the everyday.